For Elizabeth,
Daniel and Sophie

First published 1997 by
Walker Books Ltd
87 Vauxhall Walk
London SE11 5HJ

© 1997 Martin Handford

2 4 6 8 10 9 7 5 3 1

The right of Martin Handford
to be identified as author/illustrator
of this work has been asserted
by him in accordance with
the Copyright, Designs and
Patents Act 1988.

Printed in Italy

This book has been
typeset in Wallyfont

British Library Cataloguing
in Publication Data
A catalogue record for this
book is available from the
British Library.

ISBN 0-7445-3749-5

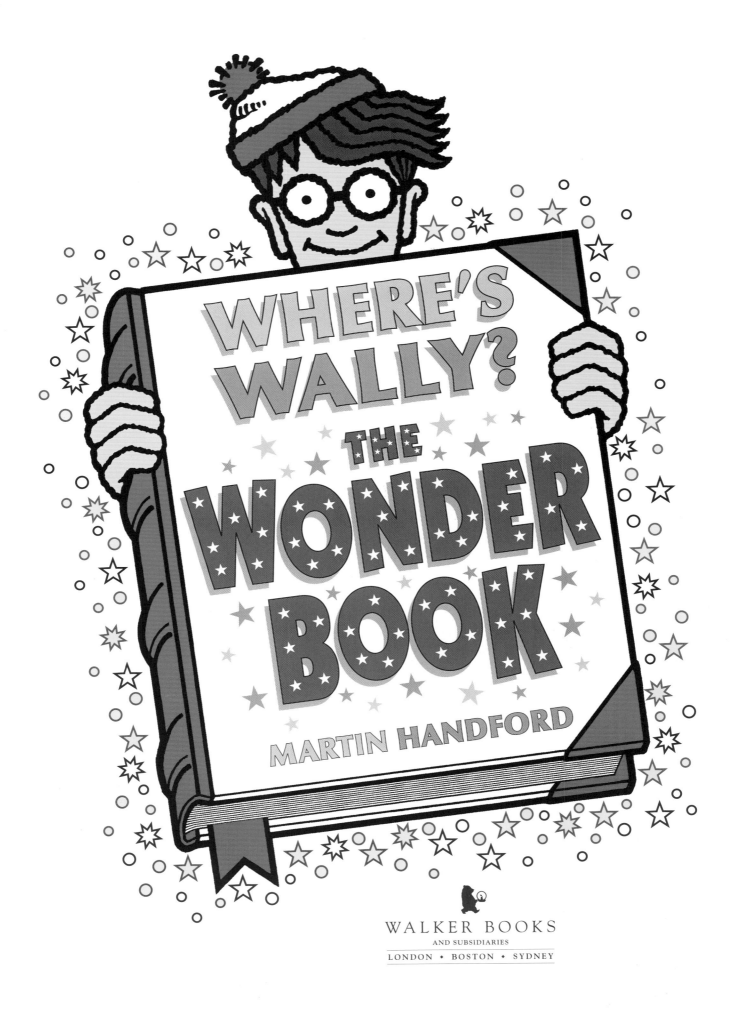

WHERE'S WALLY?

THE

WONDER

BOOK

MARTIN HANDFORD

WALKER BOOKS
AND SUBSIDIARIES
LONDON • BOSTON • SYDNEY

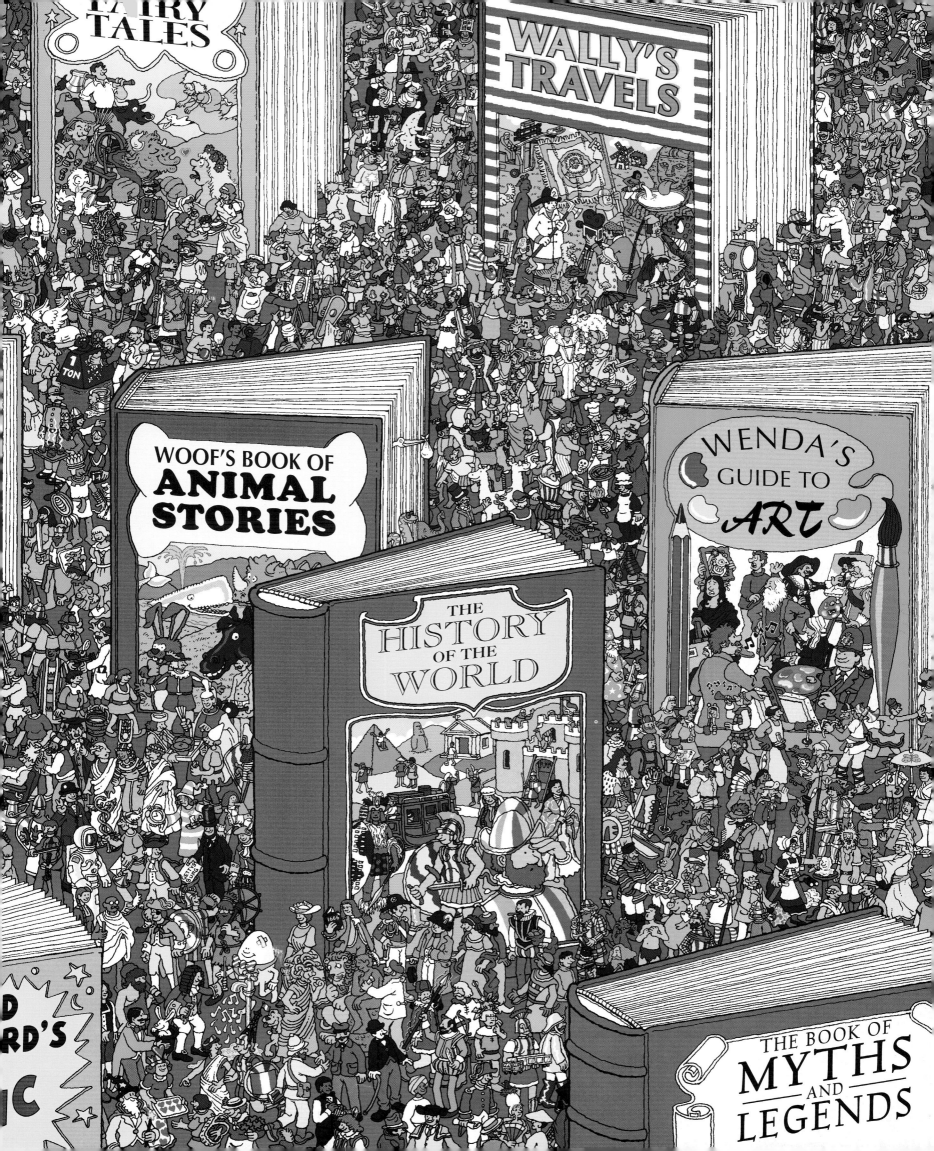

# THE MIGHTY FRUIT FIGHT

WOW! AMAZING! HAVE YOU EVER IN YOUR LIVES SEEN A PLACE SO FULL OF FRUIT? HOW SWEET IT IS TO SAIL LEMON BOATS DOWN ORANGE JUICE RIVERS! BUT WATCH OUT, WALLY FANS! THE APPLES HAVE TURNED SOUR AND THEY'RE ATTACKING ALL THE OTHER FRUIT. WHOOSH! SQUIRT! SPLOOOOOSH! THERE'S A FRUIT JAM IN THE RIVER, SCUFFLES ON THE BANANA BRIDGES AND SUGAR BEING POURED ALL OVER THE STRAWBERRIES! PHEW! WHAT A MIGHTY FRUIT FIGHT!

# THE GAME OF GAMES

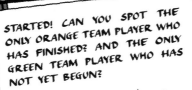

STARTED! CAN YOU SPOT THE ONLY ORANGE TEAM PLAYER WHO HAS FINISHED? AND THE ONLY GREEN TEAM PLAYER WHO HAS NOT YET BEGUN?

*FOUR HUGE TEAMS ARE PLAYING THIS GREAT GAME OF GAMES. THE REFEREES ARE TRYING TO SEE THAT NO ONE BREAKS THE RULES. BETWEEN THE STARTING-LINE AT THE TOP AND THE FINISHING-LINE AT THE BOTTOM, THERE ARE LOTS OF PUZZLES, BOOBY-TRAPS AND TESTS. THE GREEN TEAM'S NEARLY WON, AND THE ORANGE TEAM'S HARDLY*

TOYS! TOYS! TOYS!

WOW! ALL THE TEENY-TINY TOY CREATURES ARE COMING OUT OF THE TOYBOX TO EXPLORE THE PLAYROOM! THE BOOKS ARE TOO HUGE TO READ, BUT THE GREEN ONE IS PERFECT AS A FOOTBALL PITCH! SWOOSH! AND THE BOOK-MARK MAKES A BRILLIANT SLIDE! CAN YOU SEE A TEDDY TAKING OFF IN A PAPER PLANE? AND A DINOSAUR CHASING A CAVEMAN? WHAT HIGH JINKS AND HIGHWIRE ACTS ARE HAPPENING HERE! SO DO YOU THINK THAT THE TOYS ALWAYS HAVE GREAT TIMES LIKE THESE WHEN NO ONE IS ABOUT?

# BRIGHT LIGHTS AND NIGHT FRIGHTS

HEY! WHAT BLAZING BEAMS OF LIGHT, WHAT A DAZZLING DISPLAY! GLITTER, TWINKLE, SPARKLE, FLASH – LOOK HOW BRIGHTLY THESE LIGHTHOUSES LIGHT UP THE NIGHT! BUT OH NO, THE MONSTERS WANT TO PUT THE LIGHTS OUT! THEY'RE ATTACKING FROM ALL SIDES. THE SAILORS ARE SQUIRTING PINK GUNGE AT THEM, BUT THE MONSTERS SPURT GREEN GUNGE RIGHT BACK! BUT WAIT! THREE OF THE MONSTERS ARE FIRING DIFFERENT COLOURED GUNGE! SPLASH, SPLAT, SPLURGE! CAN YOU SEE THEM, WALLY-WATCHERS?

# THE CAKE FACTORY

AT THE OOZING SUGAR ICING AND THE SHINY RED CHERRIES ON THE ROOF UP THERE! THAT ROOM IS WHERE THE FACTORY CONTROLLERS WORK, BUT HAVE THEY LOST CONTROL?

Mmmm! FEAST YOUR EYES, WALLY-WATCHERS! SNIFF THE DELICIOUS SMELLS OF BAKING CAKES! DROOL AT THE TASTY TOPPINGS! CAN YOU SEE A CAKE LIKE A TEAPOT, A CAKE LIKE A HOUSE, A CAKE SO TALL A WORKER ON THE FLOOR ABOVE IS LICKING IT? CAKES, CAKES, EVERYWHERE! HOW SCRUMPTIOUS! HOW YUM-YUM-YUMPTIOUS! LOOK

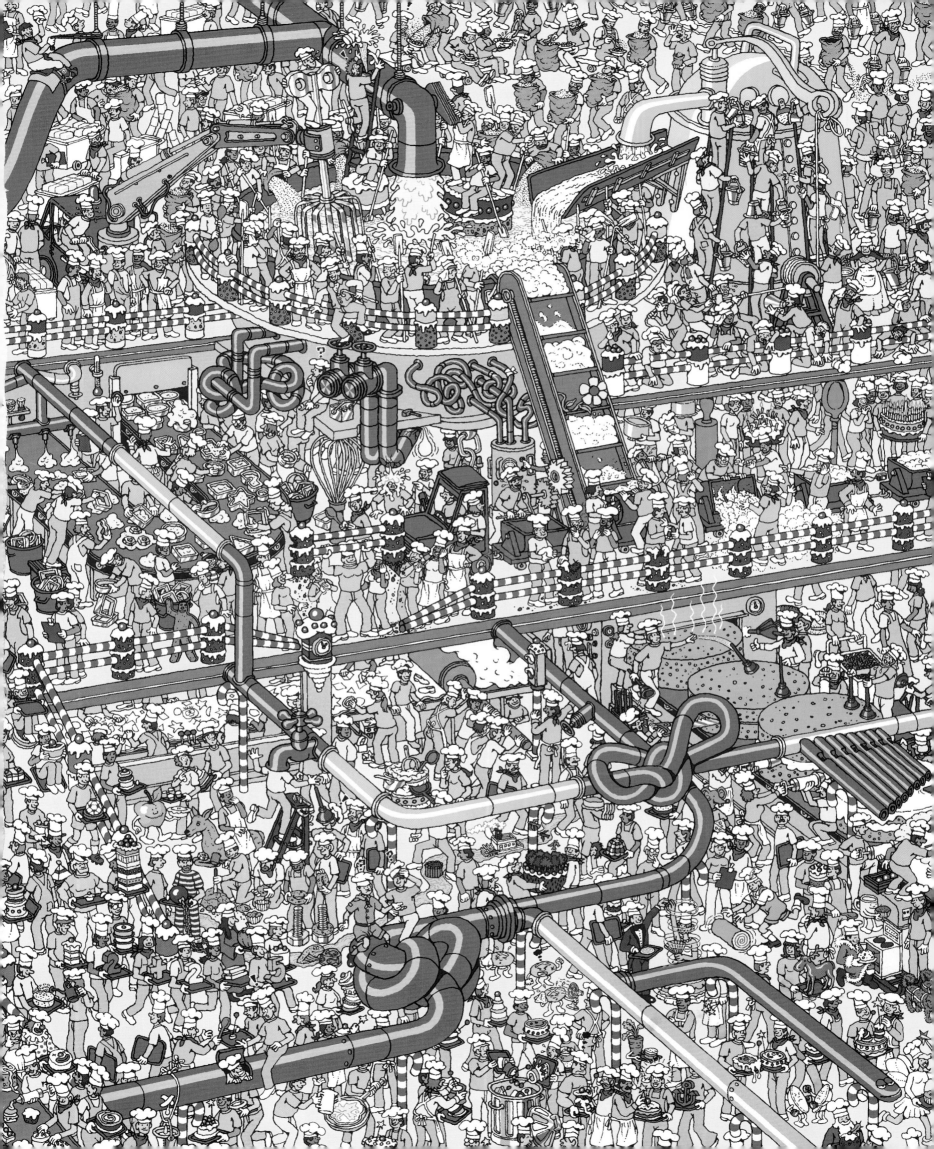

# THE BATTLE OF THE BANDS

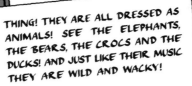

THING! THEY ARE ALL DRESSED AS ANIMALS! SEE THE ELEPHANTS, THE BEARS, THE CROCS AND THE DUCKS! AND JUST LIKE THEIR MUSIC THEY ARE WILD AND WACKY!

BOOM, BOOM, RAT-A-TAT-TAT! HAVE YOU EVER HEARD SUCH A BEATING OF DRUMS? ROOT-A-TOOT, TAN-TARA! OR SUCH AN EAR-SPLITTING BLAST OF TRUMPETS? A HOSTILE ARMY OF BANDSMEN IS MASSING BENEATH THE RAMPARTS OF THE GRAND CASTLE OF MUSIC. SOME ARE BEING PUSHED ALONG IN BANDSTANDS! OTHERS ARE CLIMBING MUSIC-NOTE LADDERS! BUT WHAT A STRANGE

# THE ODLAW SWAMP

THE BRAVE ARMY OF MANY HATS IS TRYING TO GET THROUGH THIS FEARFUL SWAMP. HUNDREDS OF ODLAWS AND BLACK AND YELLOW SWAMP CREATURES ARE CAUSING TROUBLE IN THE UNDERGROWTH. THE REAL ODLAW IS THE ONE CLOSEST TO HIS LOST PAIR OF BINOCULARS. CAN YOU FIND HIM, X-RAY-EYED ONES? HOW MANY DIFFERENT KINDS OF HATS CAN YOU SEE ON THE SOLDIERS' HEADS? SQUELCH! SQUELCH! I'M GLAD I'M NOT IN THEIR SHOES! ESPECIALLY AS THEIR FEET ARE IN THE MURKY MUD!

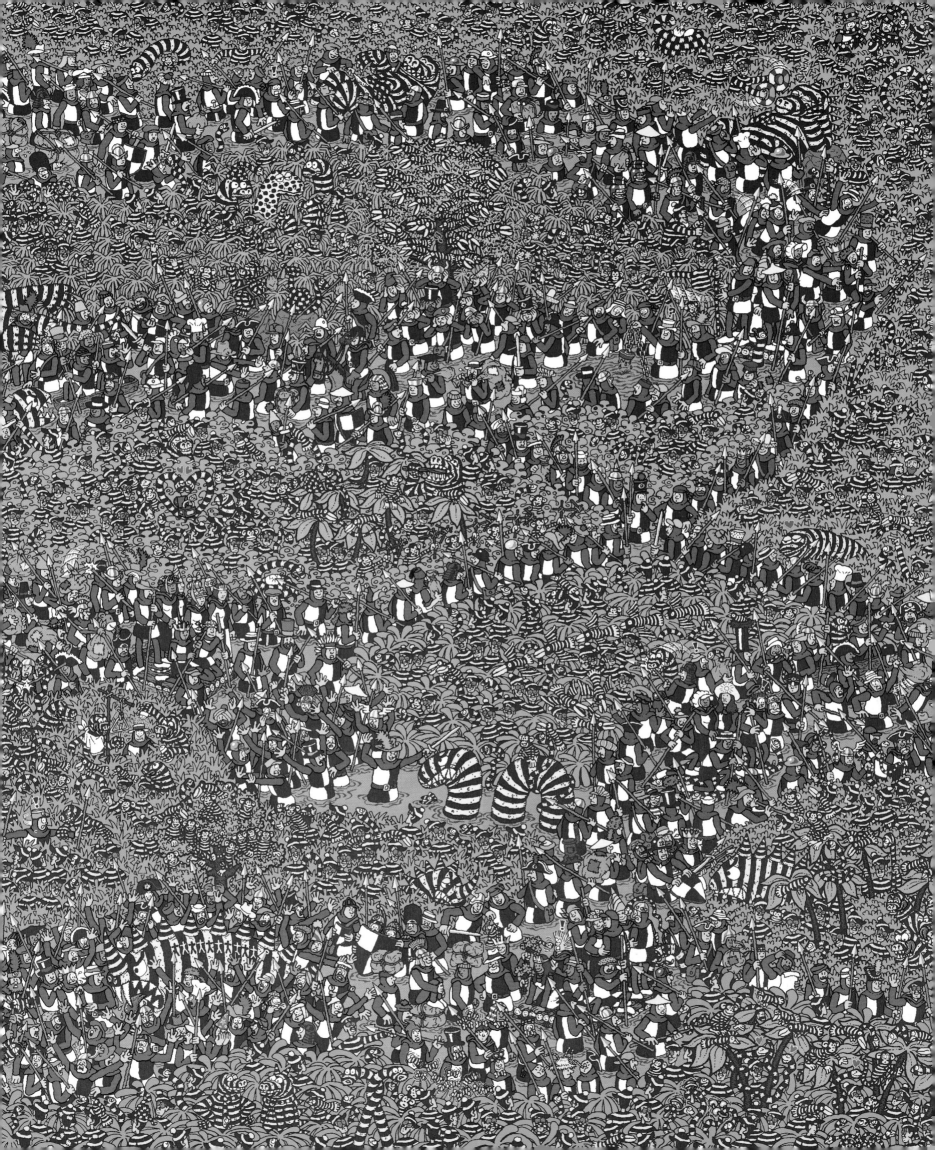

# CLOWN TOWN

CLAP YOUR FEET, WALLY JOKERS! STAMP YOUR HANDS! YOU'LL GO OOGLY-BOOGLY-WOOGLY-EYED WITH WONDER! HERE ARE HUNDREDS OF CLOWNS PLAYING PRANKS AND MAKING MISCHIEF! LOOK AT THEIR COLOURFUL COSTUMES – WITH FLUFFY POMPOMS GALORE! AND THEIR BRIGHT AND SHINY NOSES! TOOT, TOOT! CAN YOU SEE A CAR WITH ITS TONGUE STICKING OUT?

TING-A-LING! AND A BIKE WITH SQUARE WHEELS? TEE, HEE! HA, HA! WHAT HAPPINESS IT IS TO BE IN CLOWN TOWN! SPLASH! SPLAT! EXCEPT FOR ALL THOSE SQUIRTY FLOWERS AND CUSTARD PIES!

# THE CORRIDORS OF TIME

TICK-TOCK, TICK-TOCK! THE HANDS OF ALL THE CLOCKS EXCEPT ONE SAY A QUARTER TO TWELVE. WHAT A DING-DONG THERE WILL BE WHEN THEY STRIKE! CAN YOU FIND THE ONLY CLOCK THAT TELLS A DIFFERENT TIME? IN THIS SCENE ARE THIRTY-SEVEN DOORS. ABOVE EACH DOOR APPEARS THE SHAPE OF THE KEY THAT WILL UNLOCK IT. CAN YOU FIND THE KEYS IN THE CROWD, BRAINY ONES, AND MATCH THEM TO THE SHAPES? OH NO! ONE DOOR HAS NO SHAPE ABOVE IT! EVEN SO YOU MUST FIND ITS KEY!

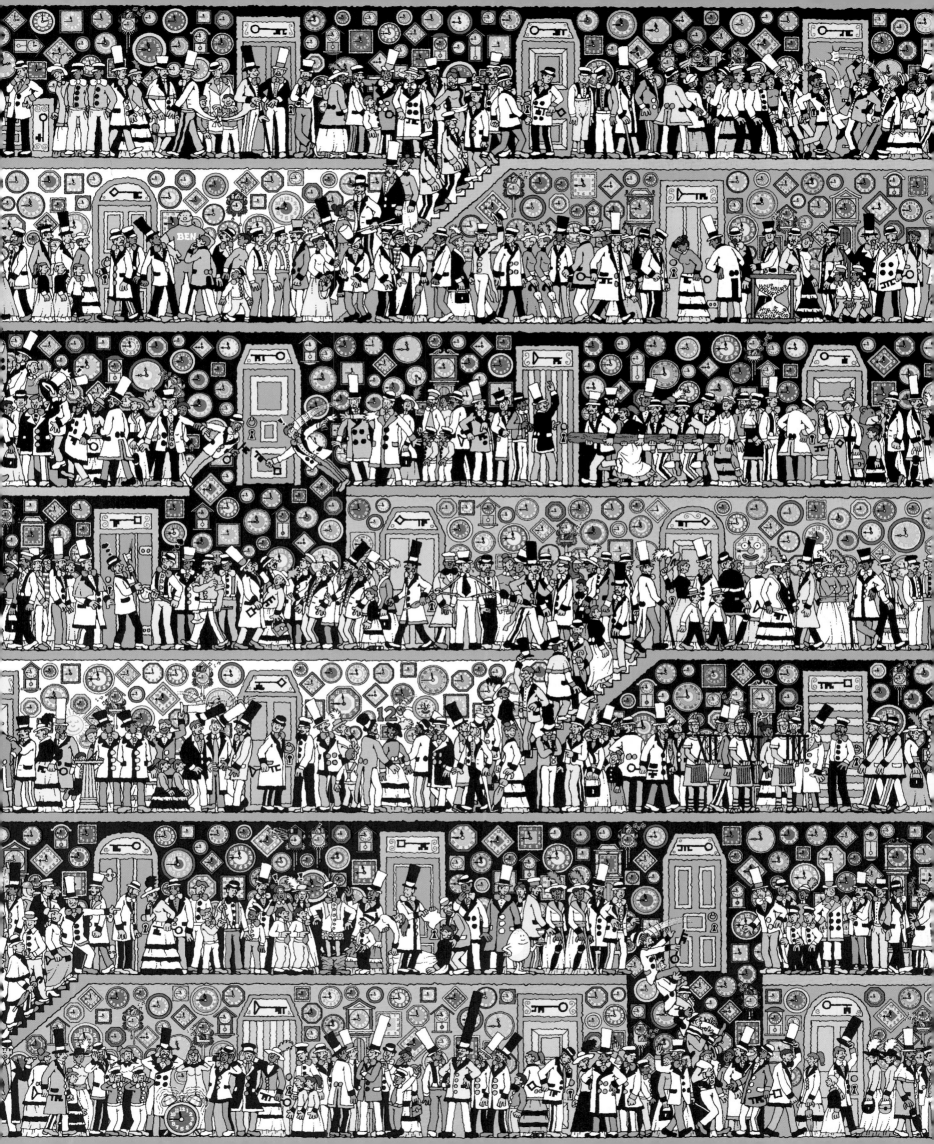

# THE LAND OF WOOFS

HEY! LOOK AT ALL THESE DOGS THAT ARE DRESSED LIKE WOOF! BOW WOW WOW! IN THIS LAND, A DOG'S LIFE IS THE HIGH LIFE! THERE'S A LUXURY WOOF HOTEL WITH A BONE-SHAPED SWIMMING POOL, AND AT THE WOOF RACE TRACK LOTS OF WOOFS ARE CHASING ATTENDANTS DRESSED AS CATS, SAUSAGES AND POSTMEN! THE BOOKMARK IS ON THIS PAGE, WALLY FOLLOWERS. SO NOW YOU KNOW, THIS IS MY FAVOURITE SCENE! THIS IS THE ONLY SCENE IN THE BOOK WHERE YOU CAN SEE MORE OF THE REAL WOOF THAN JUST HIS TAIL! BUT CAN YOU FIND HIM? HE'S THE ONLY ONE WITH FIVE RED STRIPES ON HIS TAIL! HERE'S ANOTHER CHALLENGE! ELEVEN

TRAVELLERS HAVE FOLLOWED ME HERE – ONE FROM EVERY SCENE. CAN YOU SEE THEM? AND CAN YOU FIND WHERE EACH ONE JOINED ME ON MY ADVENTURES, AND SPOT ALL THEIR APPEARANCES AFTERWARDS? KEEP ON SEARCHING, WALLY FANS! HAVE A WONDERFUL, WONDERFUL TIME!

# THE GREAT WHERE'S WALLY? THE WONDER BOOK CHECK LIST

More and more wonderful things for Wally fans to check out!

## ONCE UPON A PAGE…

- Helen of Troy and Paris
- Rudyard Kipling and the jungle book
- Sir Francis and his drake
- Wild Bill hiccup
- A shopping centaur
- Handel's water music
- George washing ton
- Samuel peeps at his diary
- Guy forks
- Tchaikovsky and the nut cracker sweet
- A roundhead with a round head
- Pythagoras and the square of the hippopotamus
- William shakes spear
- Madame two swords
- Garibaldi and his biscuits
- Florence and her nightingale
- The pilgrim fathers
- Captain cook
- Hamlet making an omelette
- Jason and the juggernauts
- Whistling Whistler painting his mother
- Ali barber
- Lincoln and the Gettysburg address
- Stephenson's rocket
- Two knights fighting the war of the roses
- The Duke of Wellington's wellington

## THE MIGHTY FRUIT FIGHT

- A box of dates next to a box of dates
- A pair of date palms
- "An apple a day keeps the doctor away!"
- Six crab apples
- Four naval oranges
- Blueberries wearing blue berets
- A kiwi fruit
- A banana doing the splits
- A pine apple
- Three fruit fools
- A bowl of fruit and a can of fruit
- Cranberry saws
- An orange upsetting the apple cart
- A banana tree
- Cooking apples
- Elder berry wine
- Seven wild cherries
- Goose berries
- A pound of apples
- A partridge in a pear tree
- A fruit cock tail
- Two peach halves
- "The Big Apple"
- One sour apple without a beard
- Paw paw fruit
- Another apple cart being upset

## THE ODLAW SWAMP

- Two soldiers disguised as Odlaws
- A soldier wearing a bowler hat
- A soldier wearing a stovepipe hat
- A soldier wearing a riding helmet
- A soldier wearing a straw hat
- Three soldiers wearing peaked caps
- A lady wearing an Easter bonnet
- Two soldiers wearing American football helmets
- Two soldiers wearing baseball caps
- A big shield next to a little shield
- A lady wearing a sun hat
- A soldier with two big feathers in his hat
- Some rattle snakes
- Five romantic snakes
- Seven wooden rafts
- Three small wooden boats
- Four birds' nests
- One Odlaw in disguise
- A swamp creature without stripes
- A monster cleaning its teeth
- A monster asleep, but not for long
- A soldier floating on a parcel
- A very big monster with a very small head
- One charmed snake
- Five charmed spears
- A snake reading

## CLOWN TOWN

- A clown reading a newspaper
- A starry umbrella
- A clown with a blue teapot
- Two hoses leaking
- A clown with two hoops on each arm
- A clown looking through a telescope
- Two clowns holding big hammers
- A clown with a bag of crackers
- Two clowns holding flower pots
- A clown swinging a pillow
- A clown combing the roof of a Clown Town house
- A clown bursting a balloon
- Six flowers squirting the same clown
- A clown wearing a jack-in-the-box hat
- Three cars
- Three watering-cans
- A clown with a fishing rod
- One hat joining two clowns
- A clown about to catapult a custard pie
- Clowns wearing tea shirts
- Three clowns with buckets of water
- A clown with a yo-yo
- Seventeen clouds
- A clown stepping into a custard pie
- A clown having his foot tickled
- One clown with a green-coloured nose

## THE FANTASTIC FLOWER GARDEN

- The yellow rose of Texas
- Flower pots and flower beds
- Butter flies
- Gardeners sowing seeds and planting bulbs
- A garden nursery
- A bird bath and a bird table
- House plants, wall flowers and blue bells
- Dandy lions, tiger lilies and fox gloves
- Cabbage patches, letters leaves and a collie flower
- A hedgehog next to a hedge hog
- A flower border and a flower show
- A bull frog
- Earth worms
- A wheelbarrow full of wheels
- A cricket match
- Parsley, sage, Rosemary and time
- A queen bee near a honey comb
- A landscape gardener
- A sun dial next to a sundial
- Gardeners dancing to the beetles
- A green house and a tree house
- A spring onion and a leek with a leak
- Door mice
- An apple tree
- Weeping willows and climbing roses
- Rock pool

## THE CORRIDORS OF TIME

- The clock striking twelve
- Clock faces
- Wall clocks
- An egg timer
- A clock tower
- A very loud alarm clock
- A travelling clock
- A runner racing against time
- Time flies
- Roman numerals
- An hour glass
- Big Ben
- Old Father Time
- Grandfather clocks
- A walking stick
- Thirty-six pairs of almost identical twins
- One pair of identical twins
- A man's braces being pulled in opposite directions
- A swinging pendulum
- Coat tails tied in a knot
- A door and thirteen clocks on their sides
- A very tall top hat
- A sundial
- A pair of hooked umbrellas
- A clock cuckoo
- A pair of tangled walking-sticks